boiling water & bleeding

bleeding

a compilation of 100 poems

lizz matthews

Michael,
my queen! you have made
my year bright, happy, and
hilarious. You've made me feel
great about myself and inspired
me. I'm so lucky to call you
a friend. I hope you love
the book as much as i love you!

♡,
lizz matthews

boiling water and bleeding

ISBN: 1530708621
ISBN-13: 978-1530708628

P.S.

*i highlighted
some of my favorites* ♡

CONTENTS

"POETRY ISN'T A HIDDEN MEANING, IT'S AN EXPERIENCE OF MEANING" - JONATHAN FARMER

DEDICATION

For Ben, Brennan, Marian and Olivia.

Special thanks to
My family
Joanna Warren
The Hawbridge School
The late Sylvia Plath & Scott Weiland

boiling water and bleeding
LIZZ MATTHEWS

1 BOILING WATER AND BLEEDING

As I slowly lower
My foot to the smooth yellow plane
I watch my foot swell in water
And the ends curl around my heel

The bottom of my foot
The gritty stripes back and forth
Of the poor pores
Being burned in my bathtub

Yet the burns are put out
Once I stay for a while
Dunked in the water
Loud pouring of heat

I stare at my legs
And keep lowering forth
Till numbness captures my body
Like an envelope of boiling water

Once I find half of myself
Engulfed in the medicine-like
Numb burning water
I cannot think at all

I feel my back
Slide onto the yellow ground
A plastic field in a flood
And I'm now going under

As I leave my nose and
My eyes
I see the diamond pattern

boiling water and bleeding

And a dark spot on my lower leg

So I pull my chin up
And water pours from the divots in my neck
A slight reminder that I'm starving
Pools emerge in curves of my clavicles

Rising up to see
The dark spot is still there
It awakens me
In a way I can't feel.

So I reach a small finger
A long nail grazes my leg
To a swollen mark of scraping
And I peel the dark mark

Picking away at the dark hardness
There is a pain but it is numbed
By numb water around me
Then I feel a slight sting

The boiling water runs
A red thread of liquid
And it is disrupted by a pouring
I'm now bleeding

The blood mixes with the water
But the boiling water grows heated
I'm suddenly swallowed
By an involuntary action

My mouth begins to curve
And I enjoy the feeling
The burning in my leg
And the red yarn-like string in the water.

Anti-gravity effects

boiling water and bleeding

My face shows a smile
But in my reflection I
Look the same as before.

Taken away
And all I can say
The name of our shelter
The name of our stay

A blank stare hides my welcoming
I welcome myself home
I welcome my guests
You have earned to be burned

Welcome, I whisper, to
Boiling Water and Bleeding.

boiling water and bleeding

2 THE LETTER

Sir,
I believe it has been a year.
A year since we met.
A year since I learned your name and went on my way.

Not was it just a year
For me, at least-
I spent a year loving,
But I won't bore you with that.

You never cease surprising me, sir.
I guess that's why write
These letters to you, I mean.
And... Others.

Some might say I am in love
That's okay...
Maybe I am,
What would you do if I were?

Will you ever read this, sir?
Will you ever write back?
Have you written of me?
That's a stupid question to ask.

Why am I even writing this?
Should I even?
I guess I'm writing this to say
'Twas a year since I fell in love with you.

3 TOO WEAK TO TYPE THIS POEM

I tell you to go
Wherever you'd like
Secretly hoping
It'd be with me
I don't want you
To feel like you have to
Stay with me, always-
But sometimes I just want you near.
I keep imagining
You stepping around the corner
Where I sit to cry
And wonder
The time ticks like a bomb
The sting in my arm gets
Clearer, harder,
More difficult to endure
I feel like I'm falling
Down off a building
The weakness pushes
Or does it pull... Me in?

I want to know I can fall
Be safe, but you were
Always there to catch me
You aren't when I need you

I feel like I could
Sink through the floor

boiling water and bleeding

Like a puddle of acid
Maybe that's what I am

The footsteps 'round
The corner beside
I hope to hear as yours
Please, please- come to me.

Catch me.

4

The beautiful pain
Stings in my soul
Like pouring the acid
Burning a hole

The pain is the love
You ink in my skin
Like a tattoo you have drawn
Deep, deep within.

The pierce in the flesh
That pours out the red
Marking your appearance
Going through my head

My lips only dream
For meeting yours
The lovely kisses
I'll save just for

5 FOR BEN

I love you.

I just thought I should say it.
I really do, Ben-
It's something I can't control.
I know I may be young

But a feeling like this-
My god, Ben
I know that it's love
I fell in love with you last year

I guess the feelings never left
I guess that they were just...
Forgotten.
Enough about me,

I'd rather talk about you-
Every time I hear a love song
I always think of you...
It's always about you.

Sometimes I feel obsessive...
I just can't hide those feelings.
I'm so happy to be happy.
This letter is for Ben

Who held my heart and kept me safe
For the years I never stopped
Loving him
Ben, I'm in love with you-

I just thought you should know.

boiling water and bleeding

I spent my life wishing,
I always knew it was you.
It's always been you.

boiling water and bleeding

6 CRY

What is it?
The blue,
The feeling it brings
To you

A sting
To the neck
Like a pinch
Removing a feather

The colors around
Convey a thought
The mixed up emotions
That build and fall

Tears feel like fire
Warm on the cheek
Boiling water, yet still
Filled with bacteria

I see life alone
In slow motion
The saddest things
Never come quick

Allowing to occur,
I'm purchasing the pain
It seems so priceless
But I'll pay anything

boiling water and bleeding

When you see me crying,
Do you think I'm beautiful then?
Once black lines stream down porcelain
Broken hearts seem gorgeous

Carry her body there
Dispose as you will
She's nothing but a pain
An obsession, a fear

Marks on her face
Suit her frame
Dusty grains colored obsidian
With no signs of snowflakes

There is no happiness here
The love he stings in hearts
Only brings one job, one love, one journey:
To kill all infected

7 WISHING

I hide this pain with a smile
A grin can convey such a message

Why do I do this?
I ruin everything, just waiting
For you to comfort and say
"No, that isn't true."

It is as true as can be
That I'm a pain, a mistake
I shouldn't have ever taken place
In the beautiful story that is your life.

Guys like you only fancy
Strong girls, with confidence
That you can trust
To take care of themselves

That is not I,
No matter how hard I try
I only feel safe
Knowing that you'll love me

I'm not forcing you
I don't expect anything
I am just constantly wishing
That you in particular

Can see me as beautiful.

8 MY LOVE

It's hard seeing you and knowing you aren't mine.
Thinking I'd never believe, hell, I don't know what to believe...
Your eyes are so difficult to see, but maybe that's a good thing-
For if I happened to look in your eyes,
I'm afraid I may fall for you.
You are, in my eyes, what I never saw as perfection-
Though to me you are my everything-
All I can see.
I heard a song once, of love- how
She is the air he breathes
Though I have heard another of how
She won't breathe him in
If you'd only take me in
To meet by the fire,
I'll show you something I never knew about...
My love.

9 SHAUN FLOYDD

Atop of the house the noise of an owl filled the streets
Beckoning, the starlight being the only thing lighting the scene
The mysterious wisps of air, cold kisses to your palms
By sweeping the top, the owl does linger
For the melancholy ups and downs of the mountains bring us
The owl's mother cries, fountains of blank emotion root
Eyes like a diamond, moon like the heart
That aches through your bones
Chilly shivers on one melancholy night
Wrapped in gauze, A rat.
Beat up in my tool box- carpentry
Look into the eyes of the owl
Feel your own heart quiver against your ribs
The hissing noises, The loud wings
Spread themselves open to the floor
Pale. Calm. Quiet. Vulnerable.
Fill the streets with the noise of an owl
And I'm safe at home
Once.

boiling water and bleeding

10 CIRCLES

He is the only one
I love him
He's the one

I never believed in love
But he had me believe
I never believed in him

I said I'd never love
He struck me with truth
"Never" shouldn't be said

When it comes to love
I'm speechless, this feeling-
I cannot describe a love in words

For once in my life
My mind can not comprehend
A thought, a feeling

He makes me feel beautiful
For the first time, forever
I trust, I love

Love isn't just idiocy
Love changed my life
His kiss means more than just a kiss

Shivers down my spine
Every time you held me
Close

Your voice plucks a string
The sound echoing my mind

boiling water and bleeding

Causing me to fall deeply, madly

The ties have been repaired
Scars left as kisses
My life has been completed

He sees me as love
As I see him, too
He is my everything
He is my love

11 NOISES

Chills down the spine
From the memories
Of painful noises

That ache in your bones
Leading you to wish
Maybe to be gone

Noises echo throughout
Your mind
Not just words but
Noises

Like they're attached to you
With a tacky adhesive
That you just cannot seem to
Peel up

I wonder how it would feel
To die...
All of the sudden,
Or maybe slowly

The thoughts that linger there
Are concrete
Slowly still drying,
Never to come up

Like at once
You cannot control
What your mind grasps
And what-

Slips by.

12 BRENNAN

As I sit on the corner
The cold bench I've settled in
I remember all of you,
I remember all of him-

Genetic mutations
Causing a self-confidence
Lacking being, dreading
The death of herself, in all black.

A man sees a car pass
It seems like it swarms
Though there is just one
She left in a car like that

There is a small girl
Who cherishes the feeling of
Her feet feeling all that is underneath
Even the hell her father brings up

An elderly woman cries
At the grave of her husband
Though she does not notice
That he never died

A lovely young girl
The preacher's pretty daughter
Worrying to be shamed

boiling water and bleeding

For her sexuality

There is a baby boy
Whom will grow to be himself
Not knowing he'll be the one
Who will change the world

Then there's a guy,
Who passes through my mind
By himself wise and kind,
Though says I teach him well.

He sees me ev'ryday
Sweetly staring, sincere-
The smile he shares with you
Can change the way you think

Through all the sadness in the world
He can brighten your day with a look
To think he doesn't see the same of himself,
I cannot see why…

He hides the pain behind his laugh
With the humor that he brings
But he'll get through it
With his cold hand on yours

With your head to his shoulder
He'll hold you close and
Hide you from the pain
We all seem to feel

His heartbeat makes you believe

boiling water and bleeding

You'll never be alone
He'll always be there
Making it better

With all the wrong things
We experience in the world
You'd be as happy as me
If you knew Brennan

13 NELLIE

Ugliness, blindness
Crimson against porcelain
My eyes to meet yours
Gone mad
The bloodstains, the agony
The hatred.
Wretched little wench they say
Calypso, Calypso
Yours to mine
Love comes from the brain
So does insanity
Fear, fear!
Nervousness aching
Anxiety- boom
Hearts to break
Feet to the floor
Yellow tip of the nail
Strike through the very
Wall
Hang a picture
Earthquake
The picture does fall
Now,
Doesn't it?

14 THRILL

"We all have issues"
We all cry
We all constantly wonder
How we will die

My issue is I love you
But not just like a friend
I'm desperately in love with you
This love just won't end

I try to convince myself
You're not all I need
That I'll never hunger
The love that you feed

I'll risk my life
I'll suffer for years
To get the love I need
The love that brings tears

My life I place
Put into your hands
I am all yours
I trust, not command

The opal ring that
Rests upon my finger
Causes me to dream up
The thoughts that still linger

Thoughts of love in my mind
Proceed to bloom
As the smile on your face shows
Lights up the whole room

My mind doesn't know what to do
It races, I can't grasp a thought
Though I see a dream, the future- nightmare
I dreamt all the love you never brought

You don't see me as beautiful
I didn't think you ever did
It had me question
All of the things you never did

My love for you hurts
You'll never love the same
But don't fear my suicide, love-
You aren't the one to blame

I can't force you to love me
If I could, I wouldn't.
Though I love you more than words can describe
I couldn't do it, I couldn't.

When you speak of love
I can only see us together
I can't be with anyone else
I won't allow it, no- never

If you could only feel
The love I find in you
My god, dear boy-
Your life no longer so blue

The happiness you bring me
I've craved my whole life
Now, my dear love,
No longer I'll cry-

15 I GUESS I WROTE A POEM

The day is black
You expected I'd say night
The oddest sensation overcomes me
Concrete running through my veins

It doesn't make it any better
She says to get over this
He says to get over myself
My bones stiffen together

All of the sudden my whole body is melted
Indulged in flames, my organs mix with cartilage
Melded together like a masterpiece
Set it on a podium and display it for them all

The darkest thing I've ever written
I can see my murder played out
I never knew it wasn't I doing the killing
Someone else behind the brush

You would've seen me as a thespian
If you had seen me at all
Pain this intense, sudden, cannot be read
just can't let it go

He says he loves me
The one with green eyes
My soulmate, he is;
Though I do not see what he fancies

I cannot control myself
I just got up
Nothing can hold me back
His shelter miles away

boiling water and bleeding

I'll run to safety before death
I do not feel comfortable here
His voice I cannot hear longer
I ache for him to be here

Can I ask for comfort now?
It will not be delivered
Why can't I feel happiness for a while
Why will you not allow me

My hand breaks
Who said it was painful?

16 THY VOID OF CANCER

Here I am praying
Not to a God nor a saviour
But for relief of a kind
Something to ease my mind

Cannibalistic seem the thoughts
They overpower and eat one another
Killing the peace
Silencing me

Invisible key on the neck
To end the sickness
Once a day or two
The spheres inked till blue

Scratched to the breast
Reddish marks like a vortex
Pulled into a darkness
Liquid lights of Loch Ness

Cracks in the skull
Paralysed by paradise
Hearts rise into your face
Yanked by heaven's lace

So here we go.
Slow, but still burning
Therapy such as chemo

My mother is submerged

17 NUMB

Aches, twitches
My arm begs for the pain
Sting, burning
My arm waits to be bled

Laid with ice
To be silenced
To cease to feel
A sensation of hunger

Eating away at
The skin that rests there
It tugs and pulls
Red and growing thin

I'm an addict
Though I have a promise
It cannot be broken
I cannot hurt him

A deal with lucifer
To bring pain on myself
No problem with screaming

I'm silenced, I'm numb

18 THE BEATING

The collar seemed to cut
Couldn't breathe,
Could hardly think

Her mind filled with shock
Fueling confusion
The pupils dilate

Sharp pains releasing energy
She cannot feel
Blood builds up

Gaps in her body
Things to fill in
Pouring health, safety

She cries for help
The beating, hands tied
What did she do

The lonely must struggle
The loners are strong
Such time to think

Bruises leak purple
A crown of gold
Moldy black decay

She is a slave
Who cares of her pain
She's human, though; feel

Beauty seeps through
You could never tell

boiling water and bleeding

She's seen as worthless

Why must you harm her
She does all for you
Harm her, do not

You'll forget her dark eyes

19 THE GAS STATION IN GRAHAM

My life search for happiness
I have found it right here
I shall die happy
But that won't be soon

Music by decades
All bad lyrics recited
Embarrassment no longer bad
The blushing through kisses

Blood no longer blue
An illusion to madness
Love through Burton
A relation like Addams

Alice and James
The beauties we'll call
And the love they will share
Together through care

We'll forget all the depression
Suicide, anxiety gone
No more panic we see
The world you control

We'll all find happiness
To be happy is to live
No goals in life
No meanings for it

While we're here,
Might as well
Let's be happy
Let's be beautiful

boiling water and bleeding

The universe we reside
Shall no longer be so sad
Love we will find
All, stopping time

20 NEVER

Kill me.
Kill me now,
For I shall not have the one I love.
He, you, will never know what I say.
What I mean.
What is it?
It's love, indeed.
Correct?
What could I ever know?
Who am I to feel
However I may be feeling
What is it that I feel?
It cannot be love
For love is idiocy,
A blindness.
How dare I love?
How dare I think I may love?
Do I love?
Idiot.
Who may have the nerve to give me the feelings
I shall never understand?
I'm blinded
What could ever be?
We may never know…

21 A NOTE TO THEM ALL

I made a promise
It were many times an offer
I ceased to keep it
I am a disappointment

I am sorry for what I've done
All the stress and pain that I've brought you
Become an embarrassment
Why should you accept me

I'm sorry I'm not perfect
I'm not the daughter you wanted
I'm not what anyone wants
That's why I attempted my own fate

I'm sorry that I'm unstable
That you cannot surely take care of me
I'm sorry that I'm selfish
I'm just trying to hide the hatred of myself

"I cannot promise anything"
That and "why" have become a motto
I'm sorry for all I've done
I love you dearly

22 WHEN I AM WITH YOU

Make me cry,
It'd be okay-
It'd be beautiful-
Though it'd be pain

My heart may
Belong to you
How do I tell?
What do you do?

How is your heart?
Your health okay?
I'm feeling sick.
But it's alright.

A true laugh
With a real smile
This doesn't happen
Everyday

Talking to others,
Well, nothing compares
I'll always be different

When I am with you

23 ACCEPTANCE

I can hear your heart beating faster
It makes me feel a bit special
Knowing that you're here always
Makes me feel safe

The feelings of love, do not blossom
They did the first sight of you
It is not new, loving you
I've felt for years on

When you hold me close
You don't pull nor push away
Almost as though you don't want me to leave you
I guess that's a possibility

I wish I could spend
My life in your arms
To rest upon you, then to
Look up and meet your gaze

The way you say hello
When you are just so worried
Don't worry, my dear
As long as you stay, I'll be alright

I can tell that you've missed me
And I don't do that to people
I've missed you, too
I've missed you so much

I never stopped loving you
I never ceased dreaming you
It's been forever, but now
We meet again.

boiling water and bleeding

I forgot how much I've missed you
Trying to forget the constant pain
Hearing your name was so painful
But now so sweet and so clear

I never thought you'd be the one
The one that would make me whole
I'll wait for you, my love
I will never lose you- no

I cannot believe you still want me here
But as long as you'll allow me,
I'll always stay near.

24 POKER

Running through
The circles of time
Tripping over couches

We ran through the walls
And fell onto counters
We thought we were one

You ruined me
And I know that I've said it
But I cannot stress it more

You just laugh and grin
Your youth running dry
A smile, a frown, a slit throat

Mommy's little puppet, I'll cut your strings

25 SEMICOLON

She has all of these words in her head
Swarming, so she wishes she was dead
Her conscience, the feelings stuck within
Constantly telling her it's "her only friend"
She skips a meal each day
Thinking all the pain will go away
Her friends try to help her up, limb by limb
And when she's about to cut she'll think of them.

26 SHOWER THOUGHTS

Paranoid
Alone at home
Small rooms with steam and fog
Getting me into a corner

Turn around, turn back
I see you there
The voice of Depression
With the presence of a person

You're pale
You're bloody
You smile
You're here

You speak
Low tone
Soft voice
Too loud

I tell you to leave
You come closer
Spitting in my face
Insulting words

I begin to cry
Giving in to you
Calling mother
Staring into your eyes

She's angry at me
And you smile at me
She hangs up on me

boiling water and bleeding

And I'm stuck with you

Dizzy and drowsy
I fall to the floor
Out of breath
Then mother's here

And you're gone.

27 CONCEAL

Terrify me
I'm used to the panic
We all attack at once

As everyone's mind is lost
I am stabilized in hypnosis
And they stumble like a drunkard

Patiently hanging from a light switch branch
Broken necks and bulbs
Astronomical solar system bastard mercury poisoning

Kool-Aid stains in a bloodbath
Was it a shot or a backfire
Burning ashy black-fire

Stunning deadly seven stilettos
Mother told me not to get a piercing
But she stabbed me in the back

28 #FMK

You know who you are
You know what you've done
You've ruined me once
You won't ruin me again

Your name is like a dagger
It hurts and it bleeds
The sore isn't all that
You've left upon me

Scars and memories
Always reminded of you
By the dark brown line
Crossed upon my arm

Death threats on your site
They're pointed towards me
I did get injured
I do everyday

The thought of you sickens me
Disgusting and fueling
Fueling my anger
I never did anything

Why must you ruin me
Not just her
All of you, that praise her-
Love her

Hurt me instead,
To please
A harlot with
A plan

boiling water and bleeding

A girl with a fire
She hides in her eyes
Full of secrets, she is
Full of lies

The bitch who killed me once
Still roams through my mind
But I'm not gone, darling-
Kill me, one more time.

29 LIMERENCE pt. 1

My oxytocin levels skyrocket
With a shortness of breath
The uncontrollable thoughts burst

I tripped about a year ago
April fifth, seeing your smile
By the sound of your voice- God help

This is called limerence
How the chemicals are released
Scientific issues, saying I love you

I suffer from this
The infatuation just dwelling
Waiting to be reciprocated

As I read and research
The symptoms...
Do I need a doctor?

It's been a year that I suffered
Yet this pain comes with happiness
The happiness I couldn't receive otherwise

The chemistry behind it
Serotonin, Oxytocin, Dopamine-
The feelings of OCD.

I do not wish to scare you
But the chemicals released
Affect like a drug

If this carries on
I may be seen as mad

boiling water and bleeding

But I'm just in love
Limerence.

30 LIMERENCE pt. 2

Nothing goes as planned
But who's to say there is a plan?
When the only thing you could ever dream
Never occurs in reality

I shake uncontrollably
It is so difficult to understand
Where is the line to separate
Likely and not at all

The stinging thoughts of love
Flashbacks of unyielding limerence
Panic attacks and loss of breath
It takes so long to recover

Why can't I be the one
Who cares not for affection
Who focuses on health
Who respects being sane

I fainted writing to you
Maybe twice, I don't remember
Psychology studies showing
This is normal, but not safe

I promise not to hurt you
I'd die rather than witnessing
Your pain- I just... I don't know what I'd do
If I ever hurt you

I wish not to harm
Such a blessing, such love
They call me limerence
A survivor of wrong

boiling water and bleeding

My tears I do see
I hope you do not
It's not like you would care
Always seeing me hurt

I don't know where I'm going
So I'll stop dead in my tracks
I'm sorry I ever harmed you
I'm sorry that I stare

31 CRIES FROM BEYOND CONTROL

Receptors repeating the motion
The same scream heard again
Maybe whispering "I love you"
A laugh fills the room

Walls are painted of grey
Hide the pink and blue
Happiness becomes sheltered
Capped over with glossy paint

Scars invisible to you
I see them plain as day
Initials were carved on my arm
Nails mark his property

Bruises from the pulling
Trust broken and torn
I cannot breathe any longer
Blissful shock; electric chair

Pure aloe, pierce, then numb
A sickening moan of murder
Gone is her immature childhood
Overcome with a new look at the world

boiling water and bleeding

32 PORCELAIN

Just wishing he was sober
Wishing it was all over
Crimson stripes across her once porcelain skin
Her mind filled with rage and her patience running thin
Starving caused by the remarks of her brother
Cutting undercover and hiding from her mother
What's she to do with useless by her side?
What's she to do with help never by?
her mind crazed with hatred filled boys
hoping one day one will bring her joy
Put in the front of the class
Oh death please come at last...
But finally they will learn a lesson
about the hell that is severe depression
A flick of a blade is how she will speak
She falls to the floor as to say "I'm weak"
Losing sight all things turn black
Her conscience says

"There's no turning back..."

33 IT'S JUST YOU

You do this thing,
I don't know what it is.

Maybe it's your laugh,
The smile you have when it occurs

Maybe it's your eyes,
When I see you staring at me

Maybe it's your strength,
Dealing with your pain and mine

Maybe it's your touch,
The cold when you take my hand

Maybe it's your smile,
Genuine and full of love

Maybe it's your voice,
The sound, I'd listen forever

Maybe it's your kiss,
That I've dreamt though never felt

Maybe it's your love,
That I see though never possess

I see your perfection everyday
Maybe it's just you.

34 DEATH, ANSWER

It just didn't work
The blades too dull
Skin too thick
To think this is all because
Of you...
The most harmless
To ever stumble upon...
Though harmless can be changed
When you're not looking
You don't see the pain
You bring to my heart
Though neither do I until.
What do I feel that you
Cannot heal?
You think nothing until
The strike of my match.
But you still do not know
Because I never tell you...
I find my love through
And in you
What is so special about
Your eyes, for which
I see but cannot describe...
Your hair, as I
Run my small hands through...
Your heart, you give
With the rest of you...
And you.
What is so special about you,
That makes me ponder
For how I feel,
That I just cannot label,
As one thing or another.
As I pay attention to every detail,

To learn more of you...
You already know all of me
How do you do?
How do you do... That?
Your mind so brilliant...
But I'd bet you already know?
Am I a sister?
Awkward, right...
A friend?
More?

You love me, you do...
Clarify as a sibling,
But why?
Do you love me or no?
But I know the answer.
You do not.
But if you were to ask the
Same of me,
I would answer like I'd
Never heard...
Because I'd never heard the-
Answer through my mind,
Easily enough to grasp it...
Survive?
Me?
In a life with you
So close,
There, to hold me...
What do I feel?
Love, or not?
Simple question,
But not.
Love me,
I'm weak,
I'm decaying.
I can't.
Any longer..

boiling water and bleeding

35 SIGNS

Just for a day
Let me hide away
No thinking, just lay
Words, no one will say
Here I'll safely stay
In a place I can hide away

36 BLEH, MY NECK HURTS

"you inspire me"

my arm is so sensitive
feel like butterfly steps

foot scrape across edges
stop it arm move

heavy right
rock weight stone stance

eyes blurry
still feel though and know

face stuck eyes twitch
tears dry smile cracks

head heavy
overwhelmed and dizzy

but despite all the screaming
i still inspire momma

boiling water and bleeding

37 LES DOULEURS DE L'AMOUR

She was wronged
Her heart was pulled-
Twas twisted then burned
Upon an ashy black hearth

Ripped through with a needle
Seeming to sew it together
But the plucking of the string
Odd pain making worst worse

She slipped in the corridor
Almost as slow as light
Her head hit the ground
The icy white plank

The whole time was painful
If you could even tell time
Constant aches, frequent sickening
She could not tell it was wrong

She was wronged
The saying of happiness
Must always bring pain
The worst pain possible

She was wronged
Though happy often
Outbursts of pain, the sting
Surgery couldn't even fix

She was wronged
To have been tricked
To have fallen
So madly in love with I.

38 TRICKS

Our love is what they want to see
Why don't we just show them?
I think I may love you, so
What do you think of me?

I see you as perfection
Though for long, the thought
Never crossed my mind
Now that I see you as you are

I believe I'm in love
But it shall never happen
I just won't let it
So how do you see me,

Though you say you love me so
Friendship is all I see you want
But is it really?
Questions covering, clouding,

Suffocating my mind.
Breathe, breathe
I can't!
You see me,
You don't,
I'm in love,
Face it,
Now-

Do you love me?

39 BEAUTIFUL

Cowardly she walks along the hall,
Covered in broken hearts and shattered dreams
Surrounded by those who shall never know her name
For she's too scared to tell.
Everyday she looks in the mirror thinking what it would be like to be
beautiful,
Realizing the only thing close to that are the crimson stripes upon her thigh
and arm.
Her only friend is a blog covered in blood splatters and empty streets.
She writes once a night to her so called "friend" before being
Dunked into a pool of medications and drowning in her shame.

40 PARASITIC

What really hurts is when
Your ribcage begins digging
Into the very seat you lean on

You wonder how long it'll last
But you know, my darling,
It will last till you die

Your body will become weaker
With signs of your bones
Piercing the limp skin that holds you together

Until you're under.
Dead, too busy decaying
Blood will drip from your cracking, dry skin

Begging to be nourished
Begging to be treated
Begging to be heard

Your tiny limp limbs will
Keep trying to hold him close
But he will leave you, my dear
He won't love you any longer.

Death is the only one that stays
and revenge
and sorrow

boiling water and bleeding

41 HAZEL LIES

Too perfect to be real
If I dreamt
Would you vanish
By grains of sand
Or like a hologram

Like one imaginatory
Perfect male
That holds me close
And sees through

Hazel Lies
Your nightmares,
I can see them
I cry over your pain

I would do anything
To keep you near
I can imagine you
Hurting me

With the words that
Sting like bees
But I'd still be happy
At least the pain is for me.

(You're my best friend.
I'll love you till I die
Please don't leave me
I die with the thought.)

42 THE MAIDEN

I annoy you, don't I?
I'm embarrassing to have around.
You don't like whenever I say bad things about myself.
But who's to say you don't believe in what I'm stating?
I pretend I'm confident to impress you.
Love, I want you to stay 'round.
You see those beautiful women and tell me you fancy,
I want you to quit reminding me if loveliness...
These maidens who float like feathers from their golden hair to their
elbows
Who's feet politely kiss the ice as they walk,
And their hips sway side to side.
Their hips to waist by perfect proportion,
Beauty, I wish I was you
The annoyance by which takes over me, I hope you could see through.
Best friend, best friend, I do love you so-
Yes, I quite do.
Indeed you see the real me.
You fancy? I wish was true.

43 "TROUBLE"

I'm writing this for you,
The one I truly love
As my heart cries out
Your name, so sweet against my lips

To feel your body so close
Even when you aren't there
I feel your strong arms around me
Keeping me feeling so safe, so secure

Though I never see myself as such,
You never cease making me feel beautiful
As I listen to your quick heartbeat
I cannot help but dream us together

I always dreamt of a perfect guy
I guess he never left my mind
For, I think of you all the time-
As you cross my mind so frequently

How do you make me feel this way?
What is it you do, so that I could
Possibly do the same for you-
Repay for all the joy you bring.

I cannot go a day
With you not crossing my mind
If only I did the same for you
I don't know, but I think not

Sometimes I feel lovesick
Like your love strikes in me
Like a dagger, straight through
The very abdomen that lay here

I hear, though see
Every memory in slow motion
The dreams I've dreamt
Of you and I, lasting forever

It is almost as if
I hunger for your love
But I do not expect anything,
I just want to know

Every time I called you "sir"
Every time you made me laugh
Every time we shed tears for each other
Every letter we kissed, though did not send

Sometimes I don't know why
When I fall in love, I
Fall off of a cliff-
Maybe it's just the cartoons I used to watch

Every memory of your eyes
When they take a glimpse at me
Seems as though it never ends
With that song playing behind

Let's leave it all
All the troubles, they'll vanish
As we forget them, forget all
I'll only focus…

Every time I try to tell you
I'm in love, I always have been
It has always been you
And words cannot describe

I write this for you
As I write all for you

boiling water and bleeding

I speak, I live for you
Now you, please listen-

44 GIVING IN

Outlets upside down
Cords tight to your skin
Slanted fans and jet voices
Metal cuts my elbow
Lone brick on a cart
Walking by and not noticing
Chiggers everywhere
Like freckles on my arms
Waiting
Lonesome
Confused
Well-aware.
Nothing is happening
But everything is moving
And I can feel it all
The world turning
Suspension
And leather.

boiling water and bleeding

45 THE LAST: CANCER, 17

I bled of jealousy
It is us who suffered
We suffer love
A plague-like virus

It usually kills
But we seemed to survive
Isn't it strange
How that came to be

White is the purity
I'll splatter wih red
In black shadows
Crying icy tears

How do you love me
How do I, breathless
Letters kissed with crimson
Never sent, never known

The light shines upon you
High degree, high passion
Heart beats, morse
"I love you"

Vision blackened
Was blurred by romance
Evil reckonings bursting
Though happy as can be

Yes, while freezing
Warmth in my heart
The bridge, we kiss
Across

46 OBSESSION, THE FEAR

What ever happened
To the rain, not coming down?
How the heart would not care
For the weather, or the sun

Resolutions to live,
When you aren't around...
Obsession, the fear
Her name so sweet

Against your lips,
Like a kiss
Her breath, when
She breathes for you, miss

Obsession, the fear

Oxygen, oxytocin-
Release, take in.
She'll live for you
She'll die for you

What is it she does?
What do you do to her?

Obsession, the fear.

47 BREAKING ICE

Rotation
Dizziness
Circles to
A line
The fainting
Lightheaded
What's occurring
When near you
Cold, the chill
It echoes on
Your spine
Pushed away
You don't know
The pain
I endure
Illusions
Illness
I'll never
Forget you
But you
Will I
Forget,
That is
Forget
Whatever
Happened
You always
It stings
But
I'm numb
Numbness
From the
Cold
You bring

73

My veins
The blood
It's warm
But not
What am
I doing?
Separating
By size
To convey
However I
Am feeling
My mind
Is numb
By the push
Of your hands
To my shoulders
The cold
Sinks in
Causing me
To feel
However I feel
Maybe hurt
But why?
Your touch?
How come?
My... Friend.

48 I QUIT.

I quit because rumors were spreading
I quit because I was concerned
I feared that if I tried again
I feared that I'd be burned

I shared to them my words of fear
I shared to them my woes
They misheard my words and gave no warn
They misheard, and mocked, and chose

I tried to clarify to refine my point
I tried but no one heard
I began to talk and I was shushed
I began to lose my words

They accused me of jealousy
They accused me of wrong
I was told what I deserved
I was told to move along.

So I quit.

49 I AM SORRY

I do not wish to offend you-
Yes, you

I make silly poems and forgot how to rhyme
I don't have a scheme, nor a theme
And sometimes I make things
that happen to offend people.

I do not wish to offend your religion-

I know sometimes that's how it seems
But really I write without thinking
And mean no such thing

I do not wish to offend my mother-

Although sometimes I am mean.
But really I just have a lot of anger
And I've never had sweet dreams.

50 THE SOUND THAT SILENCE MAKES

Hear the sound that silence makes
Then pick up your pen and write

The stinging buzz that silence makes
Pick up your pen and write

The throbbing pounds that silence makes
Pick up your pen and write

The sudden screams that silence makes
Pick up your pen and write

The unseen dreams that silence makes
Pick up your pen and write

The narrow space that silence makes
Pick up your pen and write

I am the sound that silence makes
So take out the pin
Right.

51 GONE

Crying at the sight of your name
My heart feels as though it's too heavy to beat...
Every time she whispers your name

I speak of you as though nothing hurts
Like every time, I'll simply feel nothing
Three, two, one, zero...
The ticking time bomb of my heart rate
GONE

Death says my name so sweet as she says yours
It kisses the cheek as gentle as you give to her
How she feels like she needs you
That is how death sees me

I speak of you as though nothing hurts
Like every time, I'll simply feel nothing
Three, two, one, zero...
The ticking time bomb of my heart rate
GONE

I loved you more than she ever loved you
Though you never saw me that way
Maybe if I were to just leave you
Everything might be okay

I speak of you as though nothing hurts
Like every time, I'll simply feel nothing
Three, two, one, zero...
The ticking time bomb of my heart rate
GONE

Why do you want me to stay
If I cannot live a life as yours

boiling water and bleeding

My love, I'll always be in pain
For you will always love her

I speak of you as though nothing hurts
Like every time, I'll simply feel nothing
Three, two, one, zero...
The ticking time bomb of my heart rate
GONE

So here I'll go, away
From the pain- I love you so
Though you'll never feel the same
Goodbye, my love; a message for you:

I speak of you as though nothing hurts
Like every time, I'll simply feel nothing
Three, two, one, zero...
"I'm sorry sir, she's gone."

52 THE WOMAN WITH SATIN HAIR AND SKINNED NIGHTMARES

What do you want me to do
Serve happiness to you
On a fucking silver platter?

I planned a slit to the jugular
Wounds grave-bound
Words skin deep, for a voicebox pulled through a hole in the membrane

Alice is the wonderland
Her mind was twisted
A post-apocalyptic land of forbidden fruit

Bathed in the toxins and wrapped for Valentine
Peppercorn snorted
Her in your body, in your system
It's danger
It's death awaiting

Hysteria from the blood-
The menstruated redness releasing my insanity
Emotional rebirth, flooded anger
Renaissance thoughts of my sociopathic psyche

Aurora was a sinner
In her dreams we all died as she laughed at starvation
The dictating voice flooding her victims ears
She watches as we drown in cesspools of suicide

A beautiful beast with a sickly tongue
Thorns replacing her lingual papillae
Cutting as she speaks
The words root into your skull

boiling water and bleeding

Sucking happiness through the stoma and up through the core

Her plans are a blueprinted nightmare
Hanging upon the wall of a drafting professional
A drawing of pure hatred and violence
A map towards a life lachrymose

A conqueror known for her helpless exterior
Inside she's a monster
Inside she is dead

We are all dead here
But she will never rule me

53 CUTTER

Scars are a memory
Inked in my skin
Brownish-pink marks stained
Keeping pain close

Small punctuation marks
Rest on my wrist
Indicating hatred
And a life of toxic thought

You want me to
So you can cut me
Cut her, cut her
Cutter

Hyperpigmented lines
Spotting keloids, feeling pain
You can not see my scars
Magnificent villain

The village is on fire
People shriek till death
Like exclamations will switch their future
Imaginary beings will change their minds

Words without action aren't worth it
They are as useful as my life
My suicidal notes come true
With a slice and my knife

54 CALL DR. HORDER

Goodnight, my love
My arm is cold
And I am young

Fire burning in my brain
Making holes in my temple
Aching my skull

Orbs of blue and white
Shining through an icy dust
An array of numbness

Red beads build up
Splotches appear on my skin
The paper-thin rubbery coating

My mind then settles
A freezing wind stops all corruption
Pills in a swarm, liquid stream
The wind in my mind released from the holes
And I place my head in the appliance
A hot oven for the witch
Purple seems the fate
A fiery red corruption with icy blue to stop the pain
Gasmasks of silvers-
Hansel and Gretel have met their match

55 FABRIC, ALICE, TICK, HAZARD, ENGINE, ROLLER

"Write something less depressing"
What may I compare to a mixed up mind
Attacked by a mass of depression
Personality gone by imperialism; extinct

The medicine cabinet moved
My house no longer has rope
Scissors hid behind a washcloth
She's too scared to use a knife

Frequently thinking of suicide
Doesn't mean I'd actually do it
Life is a precious gift
Don't worry that I'll end it

56 THE DAY CHRISTIANITY DIED

Black birds are sweeping over the church on this road
As if to say that the cross is a corpse
We all can see the faults in the sermon
We all know there is no Christ above.
On the day Christianity died, I was at home. I was working
That is my alibi, I am no killer
You can say I drove some to disbelieve
You can say I made them sinners
But I know what drove them into the water
A slippery slope of equality and hypocrisy
Skirts at their ankles and knives to their throats
Rage against war and they pull all their guns

Little did the Christians know
Their wrongdoings were done
The world is at silence
And we all live in peace

For this, today
This is the real heaven
And now that it's over
Call me your God.

repeat

57 SCREAM

Trust me on
My views of love
I might be young
But I've seen a lot

At the age of thirteen
Just aged another year
An older boy tricked me
Taken advantage of

He pulled me close
One thing on his mind
He convinced me he loved me,
Really, he did not.

I had dealt with depression
Maybe a year, severe
I thought he would help
I thought he would stay

He kissed me, held me
Taking me close, seeing my eyes-
He laughed when I said I loved him
For him I was just a body

I have a heart
'Twas awakened by a love
That ended in scars
It ended in bruises

I remember trying to hide
The purple,
Sitting upon my neck
And the smell of his lips upon mine

boiling water and bleeding

I tried to cover with makeup
Hoping maybe a dab of concealer would cover
The pain I would endure
And the love he lied about

You'd say it was rape
But I let it happen
People viewed me as a whore
I'd never be anything else

He didn't love me, nor care
But at least I have learned
Some love is wrong,
Some love is fake-

Hear my screams?
My cries for help.

HIS NAME WAS SCREAM

Involuntary smiles and an urge to kill
My suicide was a stinger and you were the bee
Your voice, I swear, I heard every trill
As I wrote off my fate in a promise to thee

58 HIS NAME WAS SCREAM pt. 2

I fell in love with a boy when I was thirteen

Lost in this world, I asked him to help me
Only, he wanted something more from me
Violating me was his pleasure
Every night it seemed he just wanted it out of me

Young and stupid
Over dramatic
Unconditionally in love with him

Begging, he gained consent from the girl
Ugly truth and victims guilt
Thirteen was the age the girl was changed by him

I hear myself saying no
Memories, the event never leaves me alone

Odd satisfaction from seeing me struggle
Nights of begging turned to undressing
Listening to everything he said
Yet he never listened to any of my words

The boy would ignore my opinions
He pulled off my clothes and pinned me down
I remember seeing him adjusting to the right position
Running fear through the body he penetrated
This is only the beginning, I would tell myself
Every night he will ask for more
Every night I will be forced to give it to him
Nevermind whenever I said:

"I love you but I'm only thirteen"

59 HIS NAME WAS SCREAM pt. 3

Silent screams resonate against the walls of my skull
His powerful arms hold my weakness to the bed
He puts the pressure of his body on mine
I cannot feel myself breathing

The first contact my lips had with someone else's
Sitting on his lap where he pulled me
Only I was ready
Kisses are normal couple things

Afterwards he carried me to a quiet room
Yanking me close, he whispered to me

I remember that he took off his pants
Loving the boy, I tried to act like I was...
Okay with what he was doing
Violating all thoughts I ever had of "consent"

Every weekend he would come over
Yanking me close, he would shut the door and whisper
Obviously lying, but he made me believe
Under all of the pressure, he told me

"Shh... It's okay, I love you"

60 HIS NAME WAS SCREAM pt. 4

Just in time for the rain to fall
The ocean pulled in a body so frail
A girl with red hair and a bruise on her neck
Purple marks on her skin, so pale

Opal eyes still open and full
Wet from the ocean she saw
Instead of her tears
Salt n her eyes

Red pours from the side
Bitten in water
Found after attack
Suicidal

Darkness surrounded the room
When he turned on the light
Jumping towards me
Smothering me in fear

A sudden guilt overcame the girl
She couldn't believe what she'd done
The girl took her innocence by the arm
And drowned it somewhere nearby.

No names should be said
She doesn't wish any harm
A sad little girl comes forth to say

"His Name Was Scream"

61 WINDOWS IN THE RAIN

When I looked through the window
The lights were distorted
Rain was like a sheet over a nice warm bed
And the drops moved reality

When I see the beauty of the world
Before me
It pains me to see my reflection half there

Such a beautiful canopy ahead,
Passing by
But I can only focus on a cloud
A cloudy figure hazed from her guilt

And she watches me
Her blue-grey eyes look like the windows
You can see right through the glass
See the hues of grey and deep blue outside

They make the reality distorted
Just like the drops I try to see through
That make what's inside them so painful to see
And it would pain you to see through my eyes to my mind

The windows might be there
But so many are scared to look closely
Maybe just a touch of curiosity
Could help us all

62 STARING THROUGH A DIAMOND BY THE WALL

Sometimes it gets hard to move
Like my body is heavier than a
Zeppelin
My legs are made of strong metals
And the screws are too tight

There is a strange dust in my lungs
And my face is numb on one side
My dry tongue sticks to the roof of my mouth
And my head falls to the side

I can only move my right hand
to write
Although, there is a slow movement
Of my eyelids closing and opening
Beating each other with lashes

I cannot breathe, nor think
But I feel a twinge of pain
In my arm, still
Focusing on my eyelids

There has been
Separation between the two lately, yet
When they come together
They are pooled up into
A black nothingness where
My body is numbed and
Happiness leaks onto my

92

boiling water and bleeding

Pillowcase
From my ear

I feel the poison in my gut
The toxic elixir thrashes
It's being upon the walls
Making pits and craters

As all this occurs,
I sit and wonder
Not even knowing that-

I am documenting
The scene, because

I am stuck in a canyon of
Oil the texture of lotion;
Bathing and drowning
until

There is nothing more to write.

63 McFLY, McDIE

Reverend, reverend
I'll lay out my sins
Clean out my soul
And cut the pink skin

Take me down
To a sinister place
Where I'll feel a smooth brick
Pressed on my face

Let me cry, McFly
Let me die
As I'm ostracized
From heaven up high

And pierce my back
Burn your labels on my chest
An escort to hell

And we fly to the sky
Where they cry McFly
My leader, my lover

McFly, I cry
Let me die, McFly
And they'll scream my name, McFly

"McDie"

64 THE GIRL IN GREY

Listen
Can you hear the cry of The Girl In Grey
Who haunts the places she hid away
And the height she decided to climb one day
She jumped off the tower but promised to stay
To visit us all as The Girl In Grey

Listen
Can you hear the wind her body shoots through
The air she left for me and you
I know that I breathe it, you do too
We touch the air that she once flew
And she'll fly again as The Girl In Grey

65 FEELING (,) WRONG

She was safe in a place
But there she ws haunted
She wanted a life
Where she was wanted

I am my work
Because she is not good enough
And her work can replace her
Lack of personality and worth

I'll wear a clock as a scarf
And the pieces pierce my temple
Am I feeling or not
It's not that simple

My love, am I

Feeling wrong
Or
Feeling, wrong?

66 MY GIRL, MY RIVER

As I gaze at the ripples
The river calmly waves for me
I imagine the ripples
Of her skirt, at home

The colors are vibrant
Yet her clothes are blank
But still, the thin shore
Reminds me of the thread

There are not many of us here
We are the boulders by the side
Never the fish nor the bugs
Who tear through her skirt

I hear the shrilling in the distance
I wonder if she is screaming
My daughter beat and sold
But she won't make it in the cold

The trees are broken and thin
And they remind me of her arms
The brown limbs by the side of the river
The brown skirt mother made for her

As an earthly father
I cannot look after her
I imagine god with skin dark like ours
And I doubt he is beat

When the pebbles fall in the water
I hear the coughs and I cry
I cannot help but think
My tears are most of the river

And she's drowning
My own child is sick
And I know they did this to her
The damn dams blocking her journey

As I look down the river
All I see is fog
Her future is foggy
She'll be dead by 17

The bugs in the water
The bugs in her body
She cries and yells for me
But I am not allowed to help

Imagine this
I smell the putrid smell of the river
And my daughter is sold off
Where no one will help her

The birds I see
Slowly sweep to take the fish
And a man under her skirt is gone
When the heron doth feed

Though I cannot save her,
A boulder on the side-

boiling water and bleeding

I sit and watch my beautiful river
Waiting for the beautiful hero to swoop by

My girl, my river
Your mother might be gone to heaven
But she knows your sickness
And will come by to get the fish

That force themselves
Upon your skirt
Your beautiful skirt
That ripples in the wind.

67 MATCHMAKER

All I heard was the match
As it struck the sandy trigger
And a flame arose from my finger
Awakening my soul

But I am the fire
Blowing, glowing, distorting
Blue heat burning

Counting out the memories
Crying less than never
Correcting my pain with a smile and shooting my ignorance

68 THE GRAVEYARD IS A MEADOW

I drew a line
I drew a stencil
Feeling a pen like a knife
Because I miss the sting

I miss the feeling of
Something, digging in my skin
So I drew a flower
On my arm, for a chance

As I take a small blade
And move it through my fingers
It finds my little flower
And floods it with blood

I take a picture
I want to remember my smile
For it's been so long and
Biting hasn't satisfied my addiction

I see no flower
The stencil is covered with red
And my reality turns black
As I fall to the floor, unhappy

But when I am done
I know it will be
The best work of art
My casket did see

69 HYSTERICAL

Relaxing echoes of screams
Toxic tastes of decadence
Parachuting towards the cement
But I can't pull the switch

Cauliflower mold and angel's spit
String cheese in the ear of a locust
The rooms wooden trim
Shoved in your chin

Running amuck
Cartwheels of ignorance
Ferris Wheels day off
And it rolls through the city

Shiny skin between a lap
A pen tears the skin and you bleed
A pen dents the skin and the bones
They stick out to the sky and you'll laugh

70 MY ELECTION

Lit, bit, sit
Literature is my escape to another world
Seizing the day and breaking the cold
Counting and writing away for the gold

Lit, bit, sit
Biting at my hand and wishing for pain
Another escape from feeling too plain
Shocking the echo and breaking the chain

Lit, bit, sit
Sit down at the chair
Yes, the chair right there
As I feel the bolt I'll say a prayer

How can I think of last words
When I love words so much?

71 45 MPH

She uses the tape measure as a jump rope
A noose around her neck
The gritty feeling files against
Her smooth skin

She points her toes
To the direction of the sun
Breaking an arrow
Stretching the angst

She points her toes
To the direction of hell
Breaking her neck
Stretching the truth

She uses the tape measure as a decision maker
The noose was just an idea
The gritty feeling of the dust upon
Her smooth daily pills

It happened so fast
Yet not fast at all
Little girl on a fast
Little girl's last fall

72 TO GREENLAND, WITH ENVY

Hello, my dear
Let's take a ride. A
Ride to Greenland with envy

Let's hide a few arrows
And tell them all
We can go on red

And trade me your heart
While I wander your fields
And we'll roll our carpet

Out on the pavement
Wet cement creasing
But we'll get out soon enough

And we'll rise up high
Through the clouds haze
And I'll kiss you there

But you don't want me
And I've done all I can
Till I show you what love is

He won't ever do this for you
We'll cause some trouble
And I know you

The fire in your eyes

boiling water and bleeding

Tears will never put out
And hopefully my eyes seem as perseverant

Lend me your loving hand
And we'll dance on our threads

To Greenland, with envy

73 IN THE VCR

I place my hand in the appliance
My fingers gracing the door as it springs
And the electronics touch my palm
So I stick my other hand in

I am young. Elementary.
My favorite thing in the world
My VCR
And I am curious as to how it feels

I'm a video
So I imagine my life played out
From the film on my hands
And my mommy, daddy see me

They wonder where I am
But I'm in the VCR
They'll yell if they find me
But I'm just in the VCR

They tell me I could get hurt
But I wonder and wonder
I look back on my memories
But I don't like this movie

74 PLASTIC GUMS, HILLY CURBS

In years I have learned
People with depression are more observant
So throw me out before
I adapt to your museum

Lose my mind
I'll give it to you
But don't lose it
Please lose it

There are over a thousand dots
On the ceiling in your office
I hear your voice in the background
You've repeated that 7 times

And you're working on another one
So my head shoots down
And I lost my track
But now I can see every detail of you

Send me back to school
This trips over, Ms. Frizzle
But this museum is my home
For when the chaperone loses my mind

Little piggy went to the office; little pig, little pig, let me in.

75 PROGRAM

sunrise
and a blanket fort falls
but we hear nothing
sundown

sunrise
and they build a few walls
but we see nothing
sundown

sunrise
and they smoke in the halls
but we smell nothing
sundown

sunrise
and they feed in the malls
but we taste nothing
sundown

gunrise
and i'm shot in the stalls
but i feel nothing
gundown

gunned down

76 SAVVY

Savvy, sashay
We move through the halls
Walking, talking
We laugh as she falls

Two by two
Bully in pairs
Plastic in a picture
Let's show off a little

What a nice girl
But we know all that dooms her
A secret boy sneaking in
So it makes you a whore.

She cries to me
It reminds me of the days
I see her crying from the row across
Sitting under the desk

She never knew what would become of her
What a slut
She didn't do anything to me
But I am possessed with attention

When I push her
Of course she gets hurt
But I get the attention
I just so deserve

I am beautiful
Therefore I have the right
To push her to the edge
And then she jumps.

She jumps over the edge
perhaps she took my
comments
too literally.

"Kill yourself"
I would tell her
"You don't deserve to live"
So she left.

Now Savvy, sashay
My name marks a story
And I'm blamed for her actions
When I did nothing wrong.

They threw me in jail.
Now I'll rot here
By the end, I'll look like her
But at least I got my attention.

At least she got me this far.

77 ALMOST REACHING

Almost reaching
Towards a red switch
That will instantly shut you out

I'm nauseated
I'm nauseated because I'm sick of you
Worming your way into my life
Thinking that you belong

I'm repulsed
Repulsed at the fact that you
Will run your long hands down my spine
And you know what you're doing

As I can almost touch it
The barrier between safety and pain
I grasp at my pain
When I'm gripping at my clothes

And I'm losing control
As you toss me back on the cushion
You press yourself upon me
And I'm losing control

I was almost reaching
And you placed yourself in my reach
I wanted you in my reach
But I was grasping towards a mask

And I was used
When you couldn't reach

I tried to reach for you
But you reached instead

boiling water and bleeding

With my hands
In your grips
In your cuffs
And no consent

78 EMPTY

I'm questioning myself
Up here with the clouds
Look into my core
Decide, Your side

I'm moving, soon
Up here with the colors
I'm mixing it up
Violet violence.

I'm smaller, still
Up here in the stores
The objects, my mind
Search the church.

I'm an icon, now
Up here with the stars
I'm counting like sheep
Four stars, for stars

I'm not making sense
Up here in my own head
I love her.
My heroine, my heroin

I'm bigger than life
Up here with the sunflowers
Wasting away
From the injections, infections

I'm sold away
Up here, just wishing
Support your local addict
Compile, Compost

I'm a gas.
A 90s philosophers trippy dream
Three words of the generation
And I'm dissolving

Here's my collection
Words i've jumbled
A messed up compilation
stuff I've said before.

I'm dying.
Replaced.
Without me this is nothing.
So I'll leave you empty.

79 THIS (WEAK) (WEEK)

I wake at seven
I roll out of bed and just so happen
To grab some random clothes
Throw them on, and pray I look decent

This day starts again
Five times in a row
I get in a fight with mom
Because I know how this will go

Arriving, I'll drag myself to greet her
And she'll reply with a whimper
She didn't sleep at all
But I couldn't stop living my dream

And the authority busts in with a "hello"
This happens every hour
I look around and remember
Remember why I will soon panic

A few hours from now
I'll be either shaking uncontrollably
Or not moving at all
And for this week I'm this weak

And I'll write it in my journal
The lines tell me to write without limits
And I'm getting to the best part of my poem
Not the poem that interrupts me

She knots her hair
But she is prone to an accident
And I'll smile
For the first time in this weak week

116

boiling water and bleeding

I can feel
But not feeling too much
Weak weeks are almost over
Wednesday washing weak weeks
And we'll walk

80 FOR THE LOVE OF LOUSY WRITING

You're a horrible poet.
You know that?

You can't even type
You can't even speak
What makes you so special?
Nothing.
Anyone could write one of your lines
Your mind is not different
Your mind is not special
You are nothing

You are no better than anyone else
So why do you see yourself as such?
You try to act like you are so innocent
Like you're such a damsel in distress
You deserve nothing
It was all your fault
You bring it upon yourself
It wasn't rape, because you loved him
It doesn't matter how much you squirm
You are nothing

You are asking for someone to hurt you
Maybe then you'll get attention
You're constantly waiting for someone to save you
When you are using their pains
You wish to be in the spotlight
You little idiotic teenager

boiling water and bleeding

No one loves you
No one wants you
and You Are Nothing.

81 DIAGNOSIS

post-trauma
and i'll describe myself
my mind is my patient
but i'm running low on patience

someone should help me
there's a secret me
and i'll hide her away
because i'm ashamed

deception
that's the word they pin
they pin it in
but i'm pinned down and diagnosed

post-trauma from rape
rape from the one i love
love from nowhere
and i'm going nowhere

no healing to be done
no heart to fix
i am diagnosed
with my fate

and i'm dead
and i'm gone

82 TRANSPARENCY

Too busy focusing on
The things on my mind
That run over the speed limit
Throughout it, to pass the time

To find the right words
To describe how I feel
To
Break the chain

Let me go
Lyrics in the head
With strange sounds of memories
Sitting alone with you

I can still feel you here
The boiling tears that roll
Down my cheeks
Onto the arm, I can

Still feel my grasp upon
I can't think
Of a happier place to be
Than with you

Loving me
Just seeing your smile
Makes me feel too joyful
To express in my words

They'll stumble and fall
Reaching out to only say
"I love you"

83 DAWN TERRACE

Multiple strikes to the skull
Damaging, Injuring
Making me "me"

The new me is different
I can survive
I can do anything
At least I think

What's that over there?
The cloud that floats
Around your pretty face-
Love, is it?

You're striking
Striking- strike
You damage me,
You injure me

Look at you, with
Your blue eyes,
Or are they grey?
It doesn't matter-

Strike

I saw you yesterday
At least I think
Do you remember me?
The one with the-

Strike

Can you

boiling water and bleeding

Would you
Now - Make me "me"

84 MY SIGNIFICANCE

a flashback
and i'm stuck
in his arms
he pushes

and I'm bruised
with marks of his hands
on my arms
and i'm nothing

i try to reach
grabbing at my clothes
but he's got all control
a body

yet i'm bodiless
my head was lost
and i'm here
and he took it from me

all together - i'm in a black room
cards of white fall around me
and i feel the cuts
but i'm not touched

this one spot
my finger bitten till raw
and blistered till yellow
and i'm not breathing

he pushes
a body
and he took it from me

124

boiling water and bleeding

but i'm not touched
and i'm not breathing
and i'm nothing

85 KITTEN WEATHER

Eating away the
Evening today
And the texture of
Your teeth

My tears and
Your hair
Dusty winds
Sopping wet

And I can't breathe

Under a chair
And we dance
Pose for a photo
Scratching a branch

You miss him

My baby left me
Black and scabbed
With stars in her eyes
The best shade of love

And the contrast
She blends with the grass
A black cloudy figure
And she's wrapped in a bag

I see her there

boiling water and bleeding

our porch, her Egypt
my cleo clover of luck
my patch of beauty.

86 THE BOY WHO WAITED FOR ME

I want you to be
The first thing I see when I wake
The last thing I see before I rest
I don't wish to wake
This is my dream, is it real
That you somehow love me
You are all I want
And I want you everyday
I want you all my life, sir
I fear the ones close to you
Seeking approval,
Wanting what they have: you.
A strange place we met
My second home, a stumble upon
'Twas a stage you first saw me
Strange how I could
Lay my eyes on you, my love,
And not know you're the one
You are all I want in life
You are all that completes me
Life, a broken box to a puzzle-
There is no picture to guide
Our picture is happiness
I find my joy in love
I find my love in you
I'm so happy-
You didn't let go of me
I tried to stop waiting for you
I couldn't get off of the ground

boiling water and bleeding

The sharp pains in my arm dulled
The twitching calmed as a river would
You kissed me on a bridge
The bridge was mine, from a life bad to beautiful

87 PSYCHOTIC THOUGHTS WHILE SOBER

Some whites are whiter than others
We're all too blind to color them
Acid throats seeking holes
Faithful sinners of mind

Cancel clicks
Feelings of pressure
Not feeling at all
Ink rolls the temple in avalanche

Knives attached to pencils
Pencils bend thrice more
Scars of bent wooden limp
Sicker than a dead priestess

Slight pains are beautiful
Bruises replace face-pastes
We call it makeup
I call it framework

Why does it feel like my eyes bleed
Tears imagined red and iron-like
Tastes like metal or salt
Something of grain, strain

Melt me like your metals
Taste me like your meals
Cannibalistic love affair
I never wish to harm you

Scared, afraid
The looks in my eyes
Maybe I'm a psychopath
Maybe I'm depressed

boiling water and bleeding

88 SKELETONS IN LARGE HATS

be happy
you weren't messed up before
this is all my fault
now you're at one

you saw me
you know it's what i do
to cope
don't make me seem like an inspiration

i know
what you think
convincing yourself you're depressed
but one day you will be

you can't tell what you are doing to yourself
when you want to be loved
being sad makes people comfort you
they show you how much they care

you feel warm

i'm dying, sister
i die more and more each day
don't do what i did
don't be like me

one day
you'll be watching me
you'll give me the love you gained
when they see you cry

do you ever feel bad?
you feel like you're lying to yourself?

boiling water and bleeding

lying to me
who lies in a hospital bed
look at me.
stop what you're doing.
it will be hard,
but it's better than death

89 FAIR

Why am I not equal?
Why am I treated so differently?

I require a different way
of going about things
So because of those rules, you punish me

Why am I so overwhelmed?
Why am I always wrong?

I require a different care
to prevent a relapse
So pissed about those rules, you remind me

Why am I not heard?
Why am I never allowed?

I require a different watch
on constant surveillance
So despite all those rules, you forget me

Why am I who I am?
Why am I even living?

90 POST

I guess I'll say that I like looking back on things
No matter the good or the bad
I'm obsessed with looking back
Like the trains I used to ride
The back is always different
It changes over time
Memories get mumbled
Confusion repeating itself
Her voice ices my veins
The crystals piercing the arteries
Exploding, outburst of red
It's all I see
My throat slit by her tongue
The words she made; killing
I soaked the open wounds in water
The blood blends with the bubbles
I cannot move but a chance
The thing I wanted most
She said I'd never possess
It is my own-
Sure, I'm not worth living
That doesn't mean I will not have life
I can live through you
The skin is glued

91 FIXING A BROKEN BOULDER

fighting after
my world
this morning

a shattering, glassy
grassy green beetle
and we simmer into a calm wind

i, warm, whistle through the cracks
the sound echoing through pores
it's split in half with a dead man in the middle and an axe by his side

he was an old man
he was a cold man
but his wonder took his life

as we all gaze into a coral-like structure
We cannot help but see the splits
The ashes
We'll miss it

So we gather adhesives
Paste it all on
But never caring to move

his body
The lifeless being sat before me
His teeth broken on the rock

136

boiling water and bleeding

His skull busted
But we don't move him
Because who could care for a dead man

But I knew it wasn't just this rock
The man was broken as well
But we can't fix him
So my gift
As he would give to me
Now I'm fixing a broken boulder

Like it matters, anyway

92 SPLIT, EYE, OPEN

Rustling
My fingers moving
And I observe the cracks
The divots of my skin

This
murderous music making me melancholy
Over my limbs to my hands and my thumbs
knitted, yet sheer

The line did so well
Then a curve
On the board
On the box
On the busy buzzing battles but barricading brain barriers

The warriors
Stop it

I'm in a cage
Captivated
Covered
Captured

oily blackness of depression overwhelms me

and my body falls
as I move into a calm, slow stream till I lose my
consciousness

93 ERR 404

I find a little football
I find a little sharpener
\I find myself shaking
I find myself bleeding

A little ice won't numb me
A rubber band won't cut me
Or leave a bruise
Pay my dues

And a chair breaks it
And a nail stabs it
And the blood stains it
And I am satisfied

94 TAKING NOTES

Taking notes
As he passes through my mind
I count on my arm
The times I wish he were mine

With the weakness in my limbs
I fall to the knees you once
Set your hand upon
Holding me dear to thee

It's foolish to ask why you don't feel the same
Why you don't love me as I to you
Our hearts as one would be ruthless
Why don't you see

I see those men who seem so perfect
Like obviously I'd fancy
Though I am not in the correct state of mind
It's almost madness I feel

No one could be as perfect as you
I do not see why and
I cannot see how
The love I hold so pure for you, not for any other

Is it her
The beautiful maiden who smiles a large crescent
Her eyes sparkle like diamonds
I seem like coal

Why am I questioning
Why you don't love me
It's not fair to you, it's just
Not how you feel

140

boiling water and bleeding

Black makeup smears across my face
In boiling hot tears at the temperature of a hundred
And the blood pours down the arm in droplets
From the counts of you in my mind

I stare at the beads of red building up
All of the sudden surface tension intriguing
And the streams even more
As they leave stains behind

Why am I leaving for you
Do you even deserve this
I'm making it worse
The love is growing worse

Stings in my arm that
Cease to feel, no longer feeling
Anything- no more...
Gone, she whispered, as he

Took her last note

95 PHANTOM METAPHORS

I miss the feeling of your arms around me
I went to bed with the feeling of your lips upon mine
I slept a while after,
Still the feeling stays

The thought of missing you
Resides in my skull
Permanently yours, the lingering

My body aches from the pain of you being away
I feel the blush on my cheek after you kiss it
Though it has been hours

I count the days between a kiss and a hallucination
Between a fall and a trip
Some may say love is a drug
So I guess I'm an addict

Visions and scenarios play through my mind
On repeat, they do seem
Our love is so much like a dream

You make me feel real
You make me feel beautiful
If only you were here
So I could show you what I speak

96 FRICTION

Dear Mrs. Miss
You're a bitch
I hate you more than a stinging pulsing itch
I swear you want me
To lie in a ditch
But not lie at all, bitch
For attitude's laced in every stitch
So here, give a pitch
"Oh my god, she's a witch!"
So my eyes start to twitch
I wish you gone and flip a switch
I won't miss you Mrs. Miss

But don't worry, those who wonder
She didn't die in my thunder
Nor her bones did I sunder
But sent her to a place deep under
I won't miss you, Mrs. Miss
So put me on your goddamn list
I swear you won't see the force of my fist
I just want you to know that I'm surely pissed
And that I won't miss you at all, Mrs. Miss
Sincerely, with attitude, Lizz

97 SEALING CEILING: ROOF CAVING IN

Crashing
The story's begun
at the walls of my head
They're breaking, breaking
I'm left for dead

Falling
And the girl's thrown down.
Locked in a cage, she cries
She watches herself turn into ash
as the walls start to crack

Progressing
Destruction moves from the floor,
pushing itself up to the top
It's taken so long to happen
and the ink wore it down

Breaking
Tattered walls fall onto the floor
piercing the brains first layer
A hole is torn and it starts to shed,
making its way closer

Caving
Down go the walls, broken and beat
Into the brain and into her cage
The ceiling falls into the cage,
killing her

Sealing
The roof is gone, a hole in the brain
Depression laughs as she walks past the cage

boiling water and bleeding

Seeing the body, she makes her way out
Absorbing her ink, and exiting through the ear
Depression won, another life gone. And she's off to find another victim.

98 MY BEAUTIFUL MESS

No matter how much pain
Your words hit in my chest
You know I'll always love
The boy who's a mess

He's an emotional rollercoaster
That they won't leave alone
But his pain is mine
His aches strike my bone

They'll toss him around
Like he's worthless
He's forced to believe; we'll never love
The boy who's a mess

An emotional mess
With a girl like me
No one imagined
The pair that we'd be

As he grew older
And he became a man
My beautiful mess left me
By releasing my hand

I cried and I cried
Wishing he would notice...
He came back to me, and was still
My beautiful mess.

99 MONTHS

A year in particular,
Though my life I have loved you
My life I have dreamed you
Questioning your name

Officially a month
Though my mind, forever
Infinite through happiness
Always with you

You reside in my mind
Though longer, my heart
A pen pressed to paper
Stains a love otherwise secret

It is not so easy as
ink from a pen, the
words off my tongue
They fall like I for you

Three-sixty spirals
Again and again in love
My heart beats for you
Alive, you make me

Completed now
I found you so dear
Early soulmates
Young love is too simple

A story so beautiful
A love so clear
This is real, you are real
We, in reality, fell in love

100 UNTITLED

English is an icy hell
I´m the recluse, involuntarily caged
Locked in a fit of depression
My master glares at me, enraged

You´re not allowed to save yourself
Don´t hold

ABOUT THE AUTHOR

Lizz Matthews is a student based in North Carolina. She began writing as her only outlet from her "secret world" of depression, anxiety, addiction, and PTSD. Although as a kid she claimed to love everything but writing, it became a love of hers after realizing how writing poetry could help her process, document, and survive panic attacks. She is now in what she calls the "healing process," and is still doing well through her life-long love of theatre, good friends, and of course, poetry.

To learn more about Lizz, visit her website:
lizzmatthews.wix.com/home

Thank You: A Letter from the Author

Thank you for purchasing a copy of my first book, *Boiling Water and Bleeding*. This has been an amazing journey and I am so glad that you joined me on it. Of course, the journey never ends, and I hope to see you along my journey in my next two books *Nostalgia & Night Terrors* and *In Your Cuffs*.

Writing has guided me to new heights and a new life away from what I thought was a never-ending hell. Sharing my poetry with people makes me feel great and free, and I hope that it teaches people when they read it. I hope that you look at my poems and learn a bit about people in general. How we are all such complex creatures, how we process and cope with experiences, and how your actions can shape your life. Use this to your advantage and go into life head first. Take time to learn, think, and experience.

I want you to look at poems like "Savvy," "FMK" and the "His Name was Scream" series and think about how your actions as an individual can change other peoples lives. I want you to look at poems like "Call Dr. Horder" and "Empty" and think about who the narrators are and why they're important. I want you to look at poems like "Kitten Weather" and relate to it. When you read anything, you should always think deeper. I want you to think deeper, I want you to explore new meanings, and I want you to enjoy a journey.

I really hope you've enjoyed my book and I very much appreciate you taking time to read it. Please, if you want to contact me or give me feedback, I would love for you to do so by visiting my website. I love to hear what you all thought, your questions, your comments. It would just mean the world to me. Till then, farewell.

Lizz

Visit the Wiki for Boiling Water and Bleeding at

boilingwaterandbleeding.wikia.com

And like the Facebook page at

facebook.com/boilingwaterandbleeding

boiling water and bleeding

A Sneak Peek from the Sequel, *Nostalgia and Night Terrors:*

<u>China in my Mind</u>

Watching, walking, waiting
I see my own eyes
I lose the crowd
A slow turn of the world
Dizzy, underground
I look to my side and see a man
The man has a gun, i quickly turn
I begin to drown
In a crowd deep down
Rabbit hole in Disney world
Toontown
Up and up and up in my mind
He's harmless without a weapon to be seen
And it's clearer up here
Something's not right
I don't believe my eyes
I'm scared for nothing
Paranoid panicking
For the first fluttering time
And it begins
With China in my mind

boiling water and bleeding

A Sneak Peek from the novel, *In Your Cuffs*:

CHAPTER 1

Dear future self. Hey. I'm back. Today's been pretty bad. I cut in the bathroom again, and the deal I made with the group is up to 1268. If you've forgotten about the deal already, it's when I cut because of them cutting- but four times as much. It started out as double the number of cuts but I had to change it because it didn't really seem like they cared. Anyways, I'm still in Mrs. Preston's class. I suck at it. I'm pretty sure I'm failing math. Whatever. I got a facebook last night so that I could message Brandon. He doesn't really know I exist, probably. He's a freshman in high school and he's pretty close to my... sister. Ugh. HER. but like I don't think he fancies her or anything... so... I'll go for it. I'm just worried mom and dad might find out. I hope he replies. BYE.

I closed my notebook then. Mrs. Preston began to walk in my direction.

"Victoria, will you please go up to the board and solve the algebraic expression for me please." She smirked, handing me the marker.

"I'd rather not" I answered, but she insisted, gesturing to the board. "Fine," I murmured. Taking the marker and sulking to the board. It read: $8x + 4y = -52$. I knew I couldn't do it. I slowly looked around before I touched the marker to the board. I heard someone whisper, "dumbass." I agreed with him. Laughs arose as I turned to the board.

I answered falsely.

"Now, who here agrees with her answer," Mrs. Preston began, creating a sudden silence, "Isaac, will you please go up to correct it."

"Yes, ma'am"

Well. That was my cue. I rolled my eyes at him, scoffing, then sitting down at my desk in the back. Everyone looked at me. I looked down at my planner and began to doodle. Although it was not allowed, I had created my own version of the planner, by taping blank paper to the covers and writing *West Ridge Mental School* on it- apposed to the usual *West Ridge Middle.* I also rewrote the rules of the planner where the usual rules would be. Ahem:

All patients must carry planner with them wherever they go in the hospital. Including bathrooms, water breaks, and outdoor activities. Any patient found without planner will be sentenced to straightjacket.

I must say that I am proud of myself. The bell rang. I gathered all my stuff as quick as I could, darting to the door, dodging people who either wanted to talk to me or spit on me. Sometimes both. At the same time. Luckily I got to the door- thank god. I ran to Danny immediately.

"Danny!" I called. He was standing with Ken near the door of our next class. They looked up. "Hey"

"Hey girl," Danny began. He then slapped my butt, but I didn't really want him to.

"Aye, don't do that."

"Oh come on, it's fine." He said.

"It's just what friends do, sweetheart." Ken added. They were so much cooler than me. They both had dyed hair and they were the kids your mom warned you about. Although I didn't agree with everything they do, they accept me. We walked into the classroom when it was all cleared out. I quickly did a wrist check.

"Nothing at all." Ken said, "But i did skip a meal yesterday."

"Four" I chimed in, adding the number to my log in the planner.

"You're counting meals now, too?" He asked

"Yes. Sadly, you think skipping meals is a way to get out of it." I turned to Danny. "Wrists."

"I have some on my thigh too, if you want to check."

"Hell no. Just count them yourself and tell me later." I counted the ones on his upper arm and began multiplying as I sat down up front.

"Victoria, got your homework today?" Mr. Hesner called as he entered the room. I suppose that when he saw me quickly multiplying he thought I was instead frantically filling out a worksheet. I was silent, but everyone else laughed. "So I'm guessing that's a no." He joined in with the laughter. "I'm just picking, there wasn't any homework. How are you all today?"

I begin to block it out then. Ken and Danny had been laughing. Sometimes I feel like they are using me to help them with their bullies, but that they could be on the list of mine. I guess it's okay though, I like to help. Ken is beat up everyday. He's addicted to self-harm, anorexic and bulimic, and probably the most homosexual person I've ever met in my entire life. Danny's his ex, who's bi. He's not only addicted to self-harm, but also alcohol. I'm not as close to him as I am to Ken, but he's helping me with Brandon, so, I guess he's okay. I feel like I'm overthinking. It happens sometimes, when I'm alone. It can get pretty bad... and sometimes I feel like I let it.

SUICIDE PREVENTION LIFELINE:
1 (800) 273-TALK

ADOLESCENT SUICIDE HOTLINE:
(800) 621-4000

SEXUAL ASSAULT HOTLINE:
1 (800) 656-4673

PEOPLE AGAINST RAPE:
1 (800) 877-7252